40 Leadership Nuggets of Wisdomto Live By

By

Stephen I. Nellas

This book is dedicated to my parents, Pepito and Arlyn.

I would never have learned about these nuggets of wisdom had you not had me in this world. Thanks for loving each other.

Dad, I miss you.

40 Leadership Nuggets of Wisdom To Live By

ISBN – 978-1-105-66300-0

Note from the author:

I know that you already are wise enough to become a great leader, but the fact that you have purchased this e-book tells me that you may want to become even wiser than you are now. I am humbled that you considered my book. And so let me take this opportunity to thank you.

The material that you're going to read is a collection of the lessons on leadership that I've learned throughout the years. They mostly come from many of leaders that I've come across with. Most of these lessons have been showed to me by these leaders and mentors.

I encourage you to read every nugget of wisdom for a particular day and to live that nugget for the whole day. The *Points to Ponder* portion will lead you to a deeper consideration of the nugget that you just read for that day.

So why 40 days? Why not 21, or 30?

Simple.

Yes, 21 days may create a habit and 30 days will cement that habit, but 40 days of pondering on these leadership wisdom will truly make it second nature to you.

I hope you enjoy your 40-day retreat on leadership and it is my prayer that this simple book will help you in your pursuit towards becoming a great leader.

You are a great leader.

Journeying with you,

Stephen Nellas

First Day

A leader is first and foremost a follower.

The first thing that he follows is his own word; he practices what he preaches. Following is always a trait of great leaders. The leader will not ask anyone to do anything he will not do himself. He is a person who values the principles of obedience and humility. He knows that there are people who are genuinely better than he is, and he knows that he is also better than other people in specific things.

He follows someone whom he respects.

Points to ponder:

Who do you follow?

Do you follow him because you respect him, or is it out of fear?

Are people following you?

Second Day

Leaders don't dwell on personalities when handling conflicts.

They go straight to the issue at hand and attack it relentlessly without bias. There will be people who will pull him to the sides and report things concerning the issues, but he will not be swayed by these things. He is a person who doesn't look at the persons involved, but he looks straight at the core of the conflict. He wants to be as impartial as he can be—without taking sides. He comes in as someone who is not affected by neither sides and that makes him effective in resolving the conflict.

Points to ponder:

Do you look at people when there are conflicts in your organization?

Does either side give you "inputs" regarding the matter?

Third Day

Leaders are winners. They win because they always act. Action is the weapon of winners.

This sets them apart from all the other people in the world. Leaders always look for ways to address a pressing issue. They will not sit down and just wait for something to happen. They will never delay.

Points to ponder:

Are you a person of action?

Is your waiting time reasonable or do you delay in acting?

Fourth Day

A leader thinks about the welfare of others, but that doesn't mean he fails to think about himself.

A leader loves himself that is why he can afford to love others. He has a healthy self-love that emanates from his very person. His self-esteem makes him act confidently in the midst of other people and of other leaders. He is someone who takes care of himself and does everything that would let him improve as a person and as a leader.

Points to ponder:

Do you have a healthy self-love?

Do you value yourself?

Fifth Day

Leaders give only what they themselves have. If they don't have what they desire to give, then they look for it and acquire it so that they can soon give it.

The reason why leaders give is because they have so much in themselves already. They have been nourishing themselves through constant self-improvement and self-discipline. This gives them the credibility to teach others about these things.

Points to ponder:

Do you do things to increase your knowledge and experience?

Are you constantly studying to not remain stagnant?

Sixth Day

A leader is gentle when it comes to his flock, but is tough when it comes to himself.

A leader knows that he has reached a certain level of awareness which others may not have reached yet. He knows this by heart and becomes patient with other people especially those who are still starting the journey to leadership.

But he is indeed tough with himself. He does forgive himself when he fails but he always does it with discipline. He does not go easy on himself knowing that it is just for his own good that he's doing it. He is tough with himself because he knows that he can do a better job next time.

Points to ponder:

Do you extend patience to others under your leadership?

Do you push yourself to the limit?

Seventh Day

Leaders know each of their followers by name.

The shepherd knows his flock. A leader builds relationships with his members and he invests in these relationships more than he invests in other things. He knows each by name. He invests time with them over coffee and in the tasks that they do. They receive a call from the leader every now and then. He is a dear friend.

Points to ponder:

How are your relationships?

Do you look at the tasks more or at the people behind the tasks?

Eighth Day

Leaders always have a story to tell. He connects to other people with stories.

He knows that the surest way to a person's heart is a story. Stories about successes and failures tear down boundaries and walls because these are common to the human experience. People cry, laugh, get angry, get frustrated, and even get disappointed. The leader knows this by heart and so he uses his own story so that people will gravitate to him and see him as one like them.

Stories connect people. Try it.

Points to ponder:

Have you ever used stories—even simple ones—to connect with people?

What stories have you heard from your leaders that let you make a connection?

Ninth Day

A leader is someone who knows he is actually great.

He has a very healthy self-worth and he knows that others are valuable as well. He sees the potential of other people because he has seen his own potentials in the first place. He looks at others the way he looks at himself. When he sees the good in others, he actually has seen first his own good and because he knows that he is not the only one who is good, he acknowledges the good in others.

He is not afraid to declare that others may be better than him because he is secure of himself. When others are better than him in some respects, his self-worth does not diminish. His self-worth is not dependent on circumstance. His self-worth is dependent upon his very person.

He knows he is great and celebrates it!

Points to ponder:

How much do you rate yourself as a person? A high 10, or a low 2?

Do you love yourself genuinely?

Tenth Day

The only motivation of leading is so that others will be blessed and become leaders themselves.

Leaders always want to leave a legacy. They want to continue on even if they have already gone someplace else. The joy of every leader is to see his followers improve and become leaders who are genuinely even better than he.

He wants his followers to become leaders like him.

Points to ponder:

Are you blessing others with your leadership?

Do you stunt the growth of your followers or do you encourage them to do their best?

Eleventh Day

A leader listens to what his followers have to say.

Leaders who are very effective are those whose leadership style is of collaboration. Leaders know that they don't have the monopoly of knowledge and experience. He lets his followers say what they have to say on a matter and then takes them into consideration.

But he always decides after careful examination. Whether or not he considered to follow the followers is not important. The most important thing for a leader is that he makes a decision.

Points to ponder:

Do you always say things without asking others' opinions?

Are you humble enough to seek guidance or confer with your followers?

Twelfth Day

Leaders know that they don't have the monopoly of knowledge and wisdom. He consults his mentors ever so often.

Yesterday, the focus was more on the leader's openness to confer with his followers and to allow them to give their ideas on many things regarding the organization. Today, it's all about the mentors.

Leaders know the importance of having mentors and guidance in the course of their time as leaders. They seek the wisdom of those who have gone before them and sit at their feet to soak in the knowledge and wise counsel that these mentors have to offer. This shows humility as well.

Points to ponder:

Do you have mentors for your life, career, or ministry?

Do you ask for further advice when things are not so clear to you?

Thirteenth Day

A leader has been tested during tough times. This allows him to guide those who are struggling in life by using a sure tool: the Wisdom of Experience.

Leadership is a sum total of your experiences and those of others. Leaders lead by the virtue of the experiences that they had and those that they have learned from others. Although there are leaders who had led well in spite of the lack of experience, but they still had mentors to guide them through tough decisions.

The usual thing that happens is that leaders have gone through many things and that is why they can afford to lead others by the sure path of experience.

Points to ponder:

Are you a person who has experienced hardships and victories of the past years?

Do you believe these experiences can help you lead others who may be undergoing the same trials as you did?

Fourteenth Day

A leader's circle of friends is composed of other leaders like himself.

Birds of the same feather flock together. This may sound so easy, but that's how it is. We attract people who are like us. Leaders also attract other leaders, whether they be greater or not. Leaders have many friends who are also leaders because he is the sum total of the people he usually goes out with. Leaders beget leaders. Losers beget losers. Whiners beget whiners.

You attract those who are like you.

Points to ponder:

Who are the people you usually go out with?

Are they leaders?

Fifteenth Day

A leader is a follower of other greater leaders.

Leaders humbly know that there are people—other leaders—who are better than them. They follow these great leaders like any good follower does. Leaders are always the greatest and the most loyal of followers.

Points to ponder:

Do you have heroes you look up to?

Are you a member of an organization being led by a great leader?

Sixteenth Day

Leaders see wisdom and follow it, even when it comes from a child.

Leaders do not discriminate. They only see leadership skills and wisdom. They will even follow someone younger than them if that youth proves to be wiser than they are. There are a lot of great leaders who, at some point in their lives, have followed the counsel of a younger leader.

They consider the young one's counsel thoroughly, but when proven correct, they follow it without reservation.

Points to ponder:

Have you ever heard the wisdom of a child?

Have you ever humbly considered a wise suggestion from someone younger than you?

Seventeenth Day

Leaders love.

Totally and without reserve.

They give their all and they do not expect something in return. They do things for their followers and others just because they want to do it—out of love and pure dedication. Even when their affection is not reciprocated or just taken for granted. Sometimes leaders will want to retaliate and do the exact opposite just so they could have a piece of their own shattered selves. But deep inside, the fact that they love is already a joy in itself. So they would not want to take it out on his followers or on others because he has benefited right at the very beginning.

When a leader loves, he lives.

Points to ponder:

Do you love your followers?

Do you sacrifice for them without expecting anything in return?

Eighteenth Day

There are people who think that they cannot lead others. They think that they are only great "followers".

They should read the first point in this book. In most cases, these kinds of people don't realize yet their great capacity for leading. As was said in the previous days, a leader is the greatest follower. Following well is a sure trait of a great leader.

Points to ponder:

Do you second guess yourself about being a leader?

Do you follow well and think that because of this you are just a follower?

Nineteenth Day

Leaders know that they don't know all things.

They are not conceited. They just simply know that not all knowledge can be known by a single human person. Even geniuses don't know some things about life.

Leaders are very at home with this truth. They love it that they don't really know everything.

Points to ponder:

Are you at peace with the fact that there are many other things out there that you don't know about?

Do the prospects of discovering new things and acquiring deeper or new knowledge appeal to you?

Twentieth Day

A great leader is always in solution mode.

A leader does not whine. Give him a problem and he will immediately look for ways to solve it. He is always on the lookout for solutions because he knows that the only way to address a problem is to provide solutions.

He always acts.

Points to ponder:

Do you find yourself stuck with a problem?

Do you have a bias for solutions?

Twenty-first Day

Leaders operate outside the box.

They always innovate and think of many ways to attack a given problem. They are not bound by a few ways. They think outside what is already known because they know that the things that have helped them get to where they are now may not be the ones that will let them go to the next level.

He always thinks about new things and how to improve things. He is someone who lives for innovation. He lives for change.

Points to ponder:

Do you always plan to better yourself by using unorthodox solutions?

Are you open to doing things differently?

Twenty-second Day

Leaders always strive for excellence.

For them excellence is not a goal, it is their standard. The best is good enough for them. They cannot accept mediocrity. When they do something, they do it with their all—with passion, with gusto.

They always want to surpass themselves, although they do this within the confines of reason and sensibility. Mediocrity is not a word for them. It does not exist.

Points to ponder:

Do you always strive to be excellent in all your work and in whatever you do?

Do you desire to be great in spite of the circumstance?

Twenty-third Day

Leaders know that constant practice may not make you perfect, but it does make you very good at doing a particular thing.

If there is one thing that sets the great leaders from the good leaders, that is practice. In everything, practice is the most important element, but it is also the least appreciated. Tasks are not done excellently because of lack of practice. Habits are not formed because of a lack of practice.

Constant practice will not make you perfect, but it can make you really good. Try it sometime.

Points to ponder:

Do you practice your tasks before actually doing them?

Twenty-fourth Day

Leaders know that the key ingredient to doing things excellently is by being consistent.

Leaders develop a pattern of success. They always do the things that work for them consistently and that creates a pattern in the mind and the body. Leaders who are consistent at anything, easily succeed. They cannot help but succeed even if they may want to—as long as they have been truly consistent.

When you do things consistently, it becomes second nature to you.

Points to ponder:

Are you a consistent kind of leader?

Do you always do the things that need to be done as consistently as possible?

Twenty-fifth Day

Great leaders accept failures with humility.

Great leaders are extremely humble people. They accept defeat and failures with remorse. But they almost immediately stand up to move forward from there. They will take with them the lessons that they learned from the experience and they will apply that next time.

A great leader forgives himself. He knows the human tendency of concupiscence and sin. He does not desire to fall, but when he does, he goes straight back up and then moves on with a smile on his face—a smile that only a person who is at peace with himself can have.

Points to ponder:

Do you laugh at your own mistakes?

Do you shrug your faults off and move forward with new learning and insight about yourself?

Twenty-sixth Day

Great leaders have tenacity of spirit.

They are relentless in their goals. The vision that they have actually makes them tenacious and stubborn even (in a good way). Tenacity comes from the fact that their vision of the future or their foresight is so strong that they know that if they would only persist, success will be at hand.

Faith also moves them towards the goals that are not there yet. Their eyes are called the eyes of faith.

Points to ponder:

Do you easily give up on your dreams after a couple of setbacks?

Have you ever tried not giving up? How did it feel? What was the result of you not giving up?

Twenty-seventh Day

Great leaders are visionaries.

They act because they saw something that other people have not seen. Without this vision, they will not act. Call them goals, dreams, wishes, and what have you. These things make leaders tick. It's what they live for.

Leaders have vision and they always share it with the followers so that those who run with them towards that goal will also be able to keep up and not give up.

Points to ponder:

Do you have *clear* goals?

How specific is that goal? Have you told your followers about that goal?

Twenty-eighth Day

Great leaders don't teach, they show.

They don't just tell the people who follow them what to do, but they actually demonstrate it to them. Being people who are biased for acting and doing, they will not be at ease just telling people what to do. They would always show their followers how a thing should be done. They would show them how things will go when done right.

This just goes to show that a leader will never let his followers do something that he himself will not be willing to do.

Points to ponder:

Do you show how things should be done?

Do you do ask your followers to do things that you yourself will be able to do?

Twenty-ninth Day

Leaders know how to enjoy and relax.

They know that in everything, we need to take some rest. Rest is not just a break from our many tasks. It is part of the process.

Leaders do many thinking and acting which make the body and mind stressed or overworked. That's where relaxation comes in. Great leaders go on vacations and other trips not only to relax, but also to reward themselves for a job well done.

Points to ponder:

Do you take a break in your hectic work schedule?

Have you ever gone to a vacation after such a wonderful job in the office?

Thirtieth Day

Leaders prioritize people, not tasks.

Leaders know that behind every task, behind every event, behind every office, behind every success in the company is a person who dedicated his life for this company. This connects with the day that we talked about relationships.

Relationships are very important to a leader and he will not be distracted by a stressful day or event in his life. He prioritizes the creation of deeper friendships and understanding among members.

Points to ponder:

Do your followers or member feel important in your eyes as the leader?

Are you making relationship with your followers or members a priority?

Thirty-first Day

Leaders care for people, but great leaders care for people AND tell them that they do care.

Great leaders love their people and tell them that they are loved. Leaders communicate well with their subordinates and they communicate even the affection that they give to each member. They are not afraid to honor and reward their members. They are vocal about how much they love their members and how proud they are of them.

Points to ponder:

Do you tell your members how proud you are of them?

Have you said words that build them up and honor them? How did they react?

Thirty-second Day

Leaders always listen with their mouth shut, eyes closed, and heart open.

Leaders are good listeners. They have big ears and very tiny mouths, but their hearts are the biggest part of their body as leaders. They listen to what each member has got to say. They will not interrupt often, but they take note of every word that comes from the mouth of their members.

They know that when a person comes to them for "advice" they are actually not asking for advice, but for a listening ear.

Mouth shut. While the heart and ears are open.

Points to ponder:

Are you a good listener?

Have you ever experienced just listening to a member who had problems? How did he feel after you listened to him?

Thirty-third Day

Leaders act even if others will not.

Leaders are the ones who see the vision or the goal. Because of this, they will not stop doing things that will make them delay in going towards that goal. They will keep at it even if it means that they will be the only ones doing it. They are not dependent on others. They can stand alone, but never chooses to stand alone.

Great leaders never do it alone, but as to the question of "Will they do it alone if all others will not," the answer is Yes. They will do it even if others will not do it.

Points to ponder:

Have you experienced doing something on your own alone because nobody wants to do it?

Are you willing to do it alone?

Thirty-fourth Day

Leaders are the gentlest people.

They are gentle with themselves when they fail. They are gentle with other people and members. They love and care for others more than they care for themselves. They understand failures that is why they are extremely gentle with those who are just starting their journey in life.

Points to ponder:

Do you easily get irritated with people?

What experience do you have of being gentle towards others?

Thirty-fifth Day

Leaders are always positive—they will choose to be positive about life no matter how negative it may actually be.

There is no room for second guessing and for negativity. Leaders are busy thinking about their goals and their strategy to reach those goals. Positive words come out of every leader's mouth. His thinking is always about the positive. Actions are all positive.

He chooses to be positive no matter what.

Points to ponder:

Are you a positive-thinker?

If all others are negative about something, would you be bold enough to educate them?

Thirty-sixth Day

Leaders operate by choice.

Leaders are very deliberate when acting. They do not leave anything to chance. Choice affords them great power to change the circumstances in their lives. The choices that they make propel them to achieve whatever it is that they want. They stand by their decisions because they were able to choose. They do not believe that there is no choice at all.

Everybody has a choice.

And leaders make them.

Points to ponder:

Have you ever felt trapped by things that seemed to have no choice at all?

What decisions have you made so far that came from making your own choice?

Thirty-seventh Day

Good leaders learn from their own mistakes and faults. Better leaders learn from others' mistakes. But the best leaders learn from three things: their own mistakes, others' mistakes and others' successes.

A great leader acknowledges the fact that experience is a great tool to success—whether these are good experiences or not. But because great leaders are all positive thinkers, they see the greater value of a success story. Yes, great leaders learn from the mistakes of others, but they learn more from the successes of others. They value more the tips and suggestions of people who really succeeded in the field that they are in.

They know that avoiding mistakes is good, but learning how successful undertakings were done affords great leaders quick and big strides toward their goals.

Points to ponder:

Do you read about the success stories of great men and leaders?

What are the things that you've learned from the experiences of great leaders?

Thirty-eighth Day

Leaders sacrifice for their followers.

Leaders know the value of sacrifice. Yes they know that sacrifice is always needed in order to reach and achieve a goal, but aside from that motive of success, leaders do sacrifice so that their followers and members would also learn how to sacrifice for others.

One of the greatest legacies that a leader must leave and teach his followers is the value of sacrifice. Nothing that is of great value is cheap. You have to pay the price. Success is costly.

Points to ponder:

Are you willing to sacrifice for a goal?

Have you shown the value of sacrifice to your members?

Thirty-ninth Day

Leaders give themselves totally—without reservation.

When leaders give of themselves, they give TOTAL. Everything is spent. Nothing is left. And by nothing I mean that he gives himself 100% to every task, to every meeting, to every conversation, in the relationship, in the choices he makes, in the successes that he gets. He always gives his all.

And does he lose all? No. Because as he gives his all, he will have all. The measure with which the leader gives, will be the measure that the "universe" will use to reward his efforts. He is truly wise: He knows that as he gives his all, he will receive all. That is a law of the universe that has been tested and proven true by great leaders in history.

Points to ponder:

Do you give your best to a task or for your members?

What reservations do you have that hinder you from giving your all?

Fortieth Day

Leaders speak words that honor, heal, and build up.
These are the only words they know.

They know that words are powerful. When they speak good things, good things happen; the opposite is true. Great leaders honor every person. They speak good things about everyone and they keep to themselves and to a small group of "safe" people things that might be off for them. They build up their organization by lifting people up with positive words.

They speak words that are loving, caring, understanding, and patient.

They know no other words except these kinds of words.

Points to ponder:

Are you words like honeycomb, healing to the bones?

Do you speak words that affirm and honor others?

I thank you once again for taking this 40-day journey with me. I hope you liked what you read and I hope that I helped you in one way or another.

I would encourage you to please share this to people you know. Also, kindly leave your rating and your review of this book so that others will get a heads up on what this book is all about.

You may contact me directly in my e-mail at sindwriter@yahoo.com.ph and I would be more than happy to respond to you.

Once again, thank you. You are a great leader.

About the Author

Stephen Nellas (1983-present) was born in Cebu City, Philippines, to Filipino parents, grew up in Cebu, and had his writing roots there. He started writing early in life but did not quite have the platform that he wanted. He returned to writing because he was employed as an article writer. In the course of his employment, he realized that he had to start writing for himself.

In March of 2012 he published his first ever e-book, 40 Leadership Nuggets of Wisdom to Live By. He continues to write more books for his beloved readers.

Stephen now lives in Cebu and is a prolific leader in ministry and equally a prolific thinker and writer.

www.ingramcontent.com/pod-product-compliance
Ingram Content Group UK Ltd.
Pitfield, Milton Keynes, MK11 3LW, UK
UKHW041834200726
13854UKWH00003BA/1138

9 781105 663000